Confessions

Hopeless Dreamer

Also by nieve

On Love and Life

Confessions of a *Hopeless Dreamer*

nieve

*"People do not seem to realise that
their opinion of the world
is also a confession of character."*

- Ralph Waldo Emerson

DESIGN & LAYOUT BY R. CLIFT. R.CLIFTPOETRY.COM

FIRST PRINTING EDITION, 2022.

ISBN: 9781919654140 (EBOOK), 9781919654133 (PAPERBACK)

NIEVE
@WORDSBYNIEVE
WWW.WORDSBYNIEVE.COM

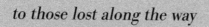

to those lost along the way

Contents
(confessions)

Success

To laugh often and love much;
To win the respect of intelligent persons
And the affection of children;
To earn the approbation of honest critics
And to endure the betrayal of false friends;
To appreciate beauty;
To find the best in others;
To give of one's self;
To leave the world a little better,
Whether by a healthy child, a garden patch
Or a redeemed social condition;
To have played and laughed with enthusiasm
And sung with exultation;
To know that even one life has breathed easier
Because you have lived —
This is to have succeeded.

- Ralph Waldo Emerson

For my mother,
not a day goes by that I don't think of you.

First Confession

I am a walking contradiction.
Half the time,
I don't know what I want.
I both love and hate
the work that I create.
I am both proud
and full of shame.
But here you will find me
in my entirety,
once again,
all of my thoughts
laid bare,
even the not so pretty ones.
I will moan a little too much.
I will forget to be grateful.
But I promise you this,
this is my truth.
And I may dream a little too big,
but I will never stop dreaming

Of the mind

The body heals,
the heart forgives,
the soul moves
to a higher place,
but the mind,
occupied,
will never let go,
and just the slightest reminder
will have the body shuddering,
the heart racing,
the soul shaking

Absolem

You are the caterpillar
from Alice in Wonderland,
aloof,
nonchalant,
puffing smoke in my face,
asking me questions
when you have nothing in your own life figured out.
So why do you get to turn into a butterfly
while I remain as small as ever,
choosing whether to take your advice, or walk away

You don't deserve the amount of time
dedicated to you
in my mind

You are my first waking thought,
my last thought before sleep
and every thought in-between

and I'm pretty sure
that when I close my eyes
you are there in every dream

Even now / I don't miss you at all / not even a
little bit / but I still think of you / sometimes
/ when I'm happy / when I'm sad / I miss the
love / I miss what we had / It really was love
wasn't it / true love / I felt it every day / now
I only feel its absence / this pain / won't go
away / my lips / they don't scream out your
name anymore / but they curl up as if you
were still here / and my body / it melts under
the sun waiting for you / I guess I'll just wait
for another you / another love / another one

Moments

When I think of love now,
I don't think of us,
I think of moments.
Moments of pure happiness.
Moments that I only realised were moments
until they were over.
I think of feelings,
of warmth,
of butterflies,
of smiles
and staring into your eyes.
I don't think of us,
I think of what we had,
what we shared,
and how those moments are still here now,
long after they occurred,
long after the love,
long after us

I spend far too long
romanticising the past
and the future
as if the present moment
is not the most worthy
of my love

Anyways

I set goals
I don't stick to,
I hate you
then I miss you,
I write lists
I never complete,
I make plans
I never meet,
I leave dishes
out for days,
I don't cook,
get takeaways

But I want to get better
and I want to change

and that is half the battle
anyways

How is it
that a space as infinite
as the mind
can feel so cluttered

Dream House

Green ivy
cascades along the wall,
wisteria
whispers around the door,
exposed brick
and muted paint,
the house is beautiful

But someone
is trying to ring the bell
and I never seem to open the door
anymore

Hardship

This world has been kind to me.
I fear it is I
who has not been kind to this world

My mind is like the sea,
parts of it are still unexplored,
even to me

I find myself drowning.
Even though I can see the shore.
Even though I know how to swim

My mumma is sick again,
I don't know how.
Why do bad things happen
to good people?
They say everything has a reason,
so tell me, what reason?
I've never seen my parents argue,
there has never been hate here,
only love.
But it is this love
that will guide us through.
Maybe that's why bad things happen
to good people,
because God knows that we are the strongest,
that as long as we have love,
we will survive

as long as
we have love,

we will survive

When I am awake,
my mind is in drive,
steering its way
over bumps and bends,
avoiding potholes,
choosing the right path

But when I close my eyes
I am no longer in control.
And that is both a blessing and disguise

I am strong,
I know that I am strong,
but sometimes I like to feel weak.
I like to feel tears
trickle down my face,
mascara staining my cheek.
I like to feel broken,
bent at the knees,
rocking back and forth,
begging
on repeat

Sometimes
it's the cause of the burn
that cannot take the heat,
sometimes
it's the breaking
that makes me feel complete

This World Without You

I know that spring
will bring golden daffodils

and that somewhere
there are choirs singing

I know that even in rain
there is sunshine

and bells
are somewhere ringing

I know there is still
music to be found

beauty
and love to give

But for now
it's hard to believe
that any of that is true

Because there is an ache
that cannot be replaced
with anything but you

I Need You Now More Than Ever

I need you now more than ever.
My hands are so cold in the winter.
My bed is so big without you.
I go to work and have nothing to come home to.
The sun doesn't rise for me anymore.
I wonder if it ever will again.
I have even stopped searching for you.
I think I just forgot.
That there is life outside these four walls.
Please strip them away.
There is nothing standing between us anymore.
There never has been.
Only my own self preservation.
But every day I'm getting older,
a little more out of reach,
and I'm afraid that if you don't come home soon,
I might give up remembering
altogether

Breaking

Some things just don't make sense.
The fact that you left
when you weren't done living,
and how
I now can't feel any pleasure
without a hint of pain,
a day of sun
without the threat of rain

But I must accept
that the sun
is not out to spite me,
that the birds don't sing
just to taunt me

I can't be mad at the world
for carrying on
though I am breaking

The way I see it,
you can either
be jealous of the sun
for its consistency
or
you can bask in its rays
and admire the fact
that it is still out shining,
even if you are not

How I'll Say Goodbye

I'll say goodbye
every night
when I see you in my dreams

I'll say goodbye
every day
when the sun comes out and beams

I'll say goodbye
every time
I hear your song and sing

And with every picture
I'll say goodbye
with the smile it will bring

And so I guess
I'll never truly say goodbye,
because your memory lives within me,
and that will never die

Grief and Heartbreak

Turns out grief and heartbreak
are much the same,
both cut you deep,
a life long pain

The scar they leave
will never close,
but over time,
the pain, it goes

Every now and then
you'll rip it open,
remind yourself
of how you're broken

Turns out grief and heartbreak
are much the same,
they stay alive
as long as you say their name

One Day

One day
the clouds will lift
and the world won't feel so black-and-white.
One day
everything is going to feel
like it's meant to be there.
One day
I won't have to question myself and
one day
this will all be real.
I don't know when this day will come,
but I take pleasure today
knowing that it will,
one day

Fashion Trends

Fashion trends
change
just like the weather,
what was in then
will come back
again.
Is this why
I cannot let go
of anything,
stacked up boxes
of precious junk
I can't bring myself
to rid,
old magazines,
birthday cards,
tales of a life
once hid.
It's been years
since I cleansed it all,
I think it's about time
that I did

Giving in to this feeling
doesn't mean
I'm going to let it sink me

I will get out of bed
for the same reason
that caterpillars cocoon,
that bears hibernate,
that the sun rises after dark

because I know
that better days are coming

Those that have known pain
know the most about forgiveness

Memories

There is a place
not far from here,
I go when I'm feeling sad,
when the world turns too fast,
where I see you
clear as day
and hear your voice
and all the things you say,
as I tell you all the things
you've missed out on,
and I get your advice
on what to get Dad for his birthday,
and you remind me
of why I love the sunshine
and how
I shouldn't be afraid of anything,
and how
death isn't all too bad,
and how
we can just be ourselves,
and how
we shouldn't even think of anyone else,
but I think of you every day,
and when I know that you're okay,
heaven doesn't seem
too far away

My mind whispers affirmations to my heart
and that's what keeps it beating

Of the body

Incomplete

Last night
I carved out cheekbones
with a chisel,
ripped up magazines
and used them as glue to hold the cracks together,
I moulded hips out of clay
and strapped them on like
buckles,
I broke bones
to finally fit into that dress,
and when I was finished,
I looked in the mirror,
but instead
of my reflection
I saw
all the things
I hate about society
pinned up
like a checklist,
each box
ticked off,
so why is it
that I still
feel
incomplete

I am a shield,
but cut me open
and I bleed insecurities

I spend hours moulding roses out of poppies,
thinking beauty is grown in rows,
cursing the wind that argues against me,
bleeding red all the while

He is a photographer,
and I who shies from the lens
would have stripped bare for him,
if it meant he thought
I was worthy enough
to be captured

— The things we do for lust

My back aches,
my bones sigh,
this body is too tired
for twenty-five

If the body is a temple,
then mine is caving in,
if the body is a vessel,
then mine is sinking,
if this body is my home,
it's not very welcoming

I am so tired
of feeling tired,
my body is screaming
at my mind

    — Do something about it

Even if a sunflower and a rose
are planted in the same soil,
receive the same amount of light,
the same amount of water,
they will still grow differently,
because they are different.
Naturally,
some will prefer the sunflower
and some will prefer the rose,
but that doesn't make either of them
less beautiful

> *— I don't know how many metaphors I need to*
> *create for myself, to get this into my head*

When is the last time
I ran my fingers over my skin
with love
instead of criticism,
when did I forget that self love
works inside out,
outside in

Note to self

Objects in the mirror
may be stronger than they appear

Slowly you are bringing me
out of this skin,
away from these bones,
this cage I am in,
slowly I am seeing
for the very first time,
my body,
through the eyes
of love

I don't know when I stopped
treating my body
as if it were anything less
than a miracle

I haven't felt the cold
since I started feeling you

Self-care is not a sheet mask / nor a bubble
bath / I hate bubble baths / It is doing yoga /
and noticing how my body feels afterwards / it
is not beating myself up for caving / it is writing
/ switching off after seven / remembering
to breathe / It is accepting myself / and not
asking for anything more / anything less

I don't know why
I let my mind bully my body
as if it belonged to someone else

As if it is not my home,
As if it were not a gift from my mother,
As if it is not capable of magic

Sometimes I see her.
Sometimes I look in the mirror,
stare deep into my own eyes
and I see.
And what a rarity,
what a divine,
dynamic
creature
she is

and how
she is everything
I ever dreamed

In hindsight,
the first red flag
was you not worshipping my body
like the sacred ground it is

The grass in my garden has grown so long,
new flowers have started to appear
and new creatures call it home

— Look at what happens if you just let things be

I think I truly learnt to love myself
when I stopped seeing this body
in parts,
things to be labelled,
and started seeing it as a whole

my body,
my entity,
me

Proof

Let stretch marks stripe
down my hips and my thighs,
let my eye bags darken
with each restless night

Give me tan lines and dark spots
where sun burns my skin,
give me fine lines and grey hair,
let the wrinkles set in

Give me skin that sags
and tattoos that fade,
I want evidence
of the life that I made

I won't yearn or regret
the days of my youth,
what's the point of living
without any proof

what's the point of living without any proof

Why did I ever care
about what this body looks like,
in the end,
it is the only thing I'm not taking with me

We are human beings,
not bodies

Of the heart

If This is Love

I watched two lovers in the park
hold hands as soon as they meet,
kissing every second,
they couldn't keep apart

If this is love,
I want it

Our eyes saw each other first,
then our hands and lips did too,
now my stomach houses butterflies,
that flutter to think of you

If this is love,
how wonderful it is

Your body is a canvas
and you've given me a brush,
we stay awake the whole night
while I colour you in

If this is love,
I never want to sleep

Our bickers turned to daily battles,
these days I don't know who wins,
but every time I open my eyes,
you're there, you just can't quit

and if this is love

I don't want life
without it

If I were a book

If I were a book,
would you read me?

If I were a song,
would you sing?

If I were a gift,
would you wrap me up
and tie with a piece of string?

If I were a dance,
would you learn me?

If I were a painting,
would you buy?

If I were anything other than who I am,
would you give us a go,
would you try?

The sun has kissed you
in places I can only dream about

Waiting

Like a flower soaking sunlight,
I opened myself,
for you to take flight

just like a bird that migrates in spring,
you left me,
a broken fling

yet like the desert that waits for rain,
I waited for you,
all the same

I left my heart in Spain once before,
maybe that's why
you were the one to welcome me back
through its door.
This city stole a piece of me
and left me with tranquillity,
but for all the wonders I have seen,
the beautiful places here I've been,
you will always be
my favourite memory

– De Sevilla

Pre -Warning

I hold anger in my chest sometimes,
I have split ends
and bags beneath my eyes.
Sometimes I don't wash my hair for days

I have a gap between my front teeth,
and a scar on my elbow
with a story
I might just tell you sometime

I have a mouth which likes to open
before my mind has time to think,
and in the morning
it takes me years to rise

These are the dark, broken parts of me.
I'm telling you now
so that you know which cracks
to pour your light into first

The Beginning of Us

You made me carbonara
and I sat on the side,
my feet
on the kitchen counter
with not an ounce of pride.
If only I had known
I was sitting
on the beginnings of love;
I would have looked
at everything differently,
like a star
watching from above.
I wish I could remember
what shirt you were wearing
and what music you put on,
I wish I knew every second
like the back of my hand
or a favourite song,
but maybe
I only need the best part,
this memory of me and you
at the beginning of our love,
and how neither of us knew

Slow Motion

Take me in slow motion,
let my arms be the ones
that wrap you up and hold you,
bring you close, I know you
have never felt this way too,
cause every time I touch you
it's like we're in slow motion,
and every movement rolls in,
rolls in like the ocean,
wash me clean and love to
watch me feel that way too,
cause baby when we're in slow motion,
this love is never ending

Let's

Let's get tipsy together
and look at the stars,
sneak into a garden,
pretend that it's ours

Let's be tourists in our town,
get kicked out a bar,
let's ditch work together
just to drive in your car

I'll take down my wall,
leave what's done, in the past,
let's do nothing at all,
and pray it'll last

This Love

I feel this love sweep through me,
like wind rushing through my hair,
I feel this love surround me,
even when I'm standing bare,
I feel this love within me,
like it has never not been there,
this love, this love you have given me,
I feel it everywhere

When I lie in your bed,
nothing could tear me away,
not work,
not my mother,
not even the promise of sunshine
after a rainy day

When I lie in your bed,
I could lie there forever,
until the sheets turn cold,
the lights go out,
no, not now,
not then,
not ever

What Love Is

How can you tell me
you don't know what love is,
how do you not see it every day,
how do you not recognise
that holding your mother's hand
is just as much love
as is
taking a bullet for it

You tell me
you don't know what love is,
I tell you
what is it
that a mother feels for her child
on his first day of school,
what is it
when an owner forgives his dog
for eating his shoes

I refuse to believe
that you can
stay up all night
talking to your friends,
phone your sister
to make sure she got home safe,
tell me your darkest secrets,
let me show you my scars
and tell me
you do not know
what love is

You Could Have Had The Whole of Me

You could have had my heart,
it only beat
when looking at you

You could have had my soul,
it had split itself
in two

You could have had my body,
those mountains swore
they would be true

Oh, you could have had the whole of me,
I was there in the palm of your hand,
but you didn't know
what you had
until it slipped through your fingers
like sand

Next Time

I felt your love within me,
I even dared to give it a name,
and now you're no longer with me,
things will never be the same

We were right at the time for each other,
but now is no longer that time,
when we were good we had rhythm,
but you leave me with barely a rhyme

When you never gave me the right answers,
I changed the questions

I should have just asked someone else

Summer Lovers

I was never
yours and
you were
never really
mine
though we
spent
summer
with my legs
wrapped
round
your chest
most of
the time
and we
held hands
in the street
and
probably
looked
like
each other's
to everyone
that we'd
meet

I play around with words
so often
until I have carved
the perfect
love
and then I expect
every man
I ever meet
to live up to it
and they never do

Time and time again,
I'm waiting on your call,
jumping at the phone,
giving you my all,
you give me what I need,
but only day by day,
and I wish I could get over it,
that the feelings
would go away,
cause even when all you do
is leave,
all I do
is stay

You tore the heart
right out of my chest,
and there I was,
thanking you for it

Mother's Perfume

I was not lonely when I met you,
I was content in myself,
but they say things happen
when you are not looking for them.
We were beautiful together,
we were lavender and rosewood,
but over time I found there was something missing,
something wanting,
wanting,
I could not place my finger.
I missed the smell of lavender,
did not recognise this new scent.
And that is when I started wearing
my mother's perfume.
I said I would never do it,
that scent belongs to her,
but the days felt longer
and I needed to be reminded of home.
I'd come back to the house
and you would be there,
but the home would be gone

I was home before I met you

I was home

before I met you

I never feared love
until we started playing it
like a game

I think of all the Friday nights
we spent bickering over tv
and how day by day
it grew into bickering
over just about
everything.
All the broken plates,
all the bruises.
How many nights
I would wait for you
to never come home.
I think of all this time
we wasted
in this state
of hate,
and then I think about how
I would do it all again
for even just one more night
of love

Your name bounces around my mind
until there are no corners,
just echoes,
all of which tell me
that I still love you

You never loved me for my heart,
but I still gave it to you anyway

Crying

I cry when I'm happy,
I cry when I'm sad,
I cry when I grieve,
or when I leave,
or if I'm mad

I've cried over films,
over songs
and silly things,
yet none of it I regret

But to cry over you
is my biggest mistake yet

The One That Got Away

I'll love again,
I know I will,
there's room inside
this old heart still

Another kiss,
another date,
another twist
and turn of fate

And one day in
a little while,
might even get
to walk the aisle

But in my heart
you'll always stay,
cause you're the one

that got away

First Kiss

You apologised, withdrew,
with a look in your eye,
brand new,
like you were guilty of stealing.
But darling, you stole me a gift.
Don't apologise, I said,
and leant in,
holding my breath,
for the very moment I had been waiting for
had begun to tumble
from my lips
onto yours,
unstoppable,
a loaded gun,
and you looked at me
and I at you
and neither of us quite knew what to do
and you told me to wait
so I did

And as I worried you were never coming back,
that maybe, cruelly
this was planned,
you returned,
with drinks in your hand,
and I realised then
that this could, would never have been
the moment that I thought it would,
and should mean

and that even if I could do it
a hundred times over
and even get it right,
I wouldn't

Because you had the same worry
spread across your face,
disbelief
that turned into relief
and then joy,
that I was the girl and you were the boy,
and I had not run away.
But no matter how hard I try,
I can (will) never run away
from that moment,
when happiness, if not love occurred,
for it is locked in time,
a brief moment when the world was mine,
and I shall (do) always look back in fondness
of us frozen under that tree,
with the rest of your life ahead of you,
and mine ahead of me

Tell Me About Yourself

Every new piece of information
I learn about you,
I wear on my chest,
proud
like a badge,
tight
like a bandage,
knowing that slowly, you are healing me,
or rather,
I am healing myself
by letting someone close to me again

Full Circle

It took time to get to know you,
time to break down my wall,
time to fall in love,
to allow myself at all

It took time to love myself,
but it was you who made me see,
that the parts I never loved,
are still a part of me

It took time to make room
for all this love inside my heart,
and I was unprepared
when in no time at all,
it fell apart

It took time to stop the tears,
fit the pieces back together,
to fall out of love,
to choose myself, come whatever

Time now to love again,
to look with an open mind,
look to see to the future
and stop looking behind

And now,
a year on,
when my heart thinks of you,
it is very rare
but always precious

Part of Me

Our love is long gone,
but I still write about you,
not because I care,
but because I cared,
and so the feeling
of those feelings
will always be there.
You may not be a part of me anymore,
but you were a part of the making of me,
immortalised in memory,
and now, in poetry

Opportunity of Love

You awoke my heart
with soft brush strokes,
rekindled that feeling,
that glow
of possibility,
and I think if I had stayed
longer than these three days
I would have fallen
deep in love
and inevitable heartbreak,
when inevitably,
I'd have to leave,
because this could never be permanent.
Two hearts need one home,
I learnt that long ago,
and long distance
is never worth the dance.
But thank you for that opportunity
of love,
even if
it never stood a chance

Of the soul

Water Baby

I am a water baby,
always have been,
take me to the ocean
over the forest
any day,
leave me salty,
windswept,
I was born
to be that way.
No wonder water
so often pools
between my legs,
no wonder I have yet
to explore
all of my depths,
no wonder I don't fall in love,
I drown in it,
and no wonder the love never really leaves,
it just gets lost inside of me

Time

I need to borrow time / from another place / another life / I just need it / I need it to survive / I need it to love / I need it to thrive / I need it to find / find what I've been looking for / even if I don't know what that is yet / there just never seems to be enough / and the days come rolling in / slow barrels of waves / and each wave turns to another day / but even borrowed time could never be enough / I have too much love to give / too many people to love / too many lives to live / even if I had all the time in the world / would I be able to leave a mark / how could I ensure that I survive / ensure the love survives / when all I am is water and earth and air / all of which I borrow

How Many Lives Have I Lived

How many lives have I lived,
my skin is young
but my soul is weathered,
the stars call me
like old friends
but the hills remind me
there is time yet.
How many lives do I have to live
when this one wears thin
like my favourite cardigan,
full of comfort,
holding me in.
But does it matter where I go
or does it matter where I've been,
consequence is nothing
without sin
and when one life ends,
another has chance
to begin

What's here today
is gone tomorrow,
spring has come
to winter's sorrow,
I came and lost
and now I'm hollow,
that smile of yours
I'll have to borrow

Over Easy

I've always been
a little over easy

People always seem
to add a pinch more salt

Over seasoned
in heart-break

and undercooked
in love

A little too spicy
for some,
not spicy enough
for others

Maybe I should just focus
on feeding myself

WOMAN

I am ocean
waves
and shore

I am wind
shelter
and storm

I am lightning
thunder
and rain

I am woman,
I'll rise again

Conversation With The Stars

Last night I had a conversation
with the stars,
I asked them
what happens to life
when it is no longer ours

They said they didn't know,
that all they know is hearts,
and that they still beat
though broken
into parts

And so I thought,
so too must the soul
continue to be
if lost
and not whole

Every Day Like This

We should sing and laugh
and cry if we want

Life will carry on
even if we don't

And we should dance, get high,
try and reach the stars

and treat the world
as if it's all ours

No day
should be lived
without a little music

No life
should be lived
without love

And I could live
every day like this,
wearing happiness
like a glove

No day should be lived

without a little music

No life should be lived

without love

Happiness

I know it lives inside of me
somewhere,
golden,
shining,
and one day,
like the sun,
it will rise,
as if it always has,
as if it never stopped,
and the sky
will be bright
and the clouds
will be lifted
and my soul
will beam
from the inside

When I complete a poem,
my body has birthed the words,
every fibre of my being glows,
and that is what tells me
that though I'm far from perfect
I'm doing something right

Everyday Magic

I hear your voice
when I'm about to drop my clothes
in a pile on the floor.
I wear your ring every day
and sometimes the diamonds catch the sun
and they glimmer.
I see white flowers everywhere I go.
My sister flicks her hair
and years of memories flash back
in a second.
Strangers smell my perfume
and compliment me on it.
I get these weird moments of bravery
sometimes.
Sometimes
your song is playing
when I turn on the radio.
That's how I know it's true.
That souls live among us.
What else could cause such magic
but you

Loss

None of this taught me
that life is short,
you have to live it.
That's fucking obvious.
You have to love it.
You have to love it,
you have to love it,
you have to love it.
You have to love things,
love people,
love them deeply.
You have to accept things.
You have to accept that life
will find its way
around you.
That things are a result of actions.
That's why you have to be kind, always.
Live, not recklessly, but bravely,
and make sure you are alive
every day that you live

We must not be ungrateful
for the cards
we have been dealt,
at least they let us play the game

A Life Worth Living

To have money,
to have success,
to have fame

To spend your time
chasing a single gain

What a life to live,
what a game to play

But to feel joy in singing,
to notice the smell
of roses in a wild garden

To see new stories
in paths known so well

To hear love in the wind

Now that is a life
truly worth living

Love
(After Alex Dimitrov)

I love all types of laughter

Belly laughter

Silent laughter

A stranger's laughter

I just love strangers

I love anyone that ever speaks in public

I love performances and the idea that you can be someone else

I love fake names and nicknames

I love when I get to pet someone else's dog

I love seeing people hold hands in public

I especially love thumb caresses

I just love love

I love that we continue to love after having our hearts broken

I love that I see love everywhere I go

I love going to new places

I love slow travel

I love taking photographs

I love discovering new places in familiar places

I love getting ready to go out

But equally I love coming home after a night out

I love coming home to myself

I love my past and my future

I am learning to love my present

I love the idea that love lasts forever

I love deep conversations

I love how there are always new things to say

But I also love silence

I love the feeling after doing that thing you were
dreading

I love that eventually the day always comes

And I love that I will always do it, whatever it is,
when it's due

I love when people are passionate about their jobs

I love red underwear

I love how everyone is naked at some point every
single day

I love when shops have loyalty cards and I love
using them

I love getting actual tickets instead of e-tickets

I love getting to the front of a long queue

I love when words keep me up at night

I love lists

I love playlists

Especially other people's

I love that there are so many different types of
music and I love listening to them all

I love that other languages have multiple ways of
saying love but in English there is just one

I love that there are a million ways you can show
someone you love them instead

I love when people say bless you after you sneeze
but they don't know what to say when you hiccup

I love unwritten rules in society

I love the ways we congratulate each other

I love watching someone open their presents

I love watching someone watching a movie

I love supermarkets in foreign countries

I love people who go to museums alone

But most of all,

I love that there are countless things to love,

if you start counting

If you are what you love
(After Skyler Saunders)

If you are what you love then I am
kitchen dancing,
barefoot beach walks
and singing in the rain,
I am two shots of strong coffee,
milk and no sugar,
from one of those side street cafés
in Spain,
I am all love and no hate,
I am inspiration,
I am dreams,
I'm both the sun
and the moon
and exist only in extremes.
If you are what you love
then I'd be no one else but me
cause I am the words on this page
I am poetry

When we make love
we are not bodies,
but souls,
we are artists
making music
for one another,
forever listening,
playing,
songs we've never heard,
but we don't need
to guess the words

I have found a place
to rest my bones
in this silent palace
of unfamiliarity.
I have found it in the trees,
en los sonidos,
in the breeze,
and though I do not know
these walls,
I know I will see them
in my dreams,
and there,
I can call them home

— *Palacio de los sueños*

So This Is What It's Like

So this is what it's like
to feel the sun from the inside out,
to take a deep breath
and feel it in the soul.
I don't think I've ever felt so calm.
I guess thoughts can just be thoughts.
They don't need to stay

I think of work,
commitments,
problems,
but for the first time,
they do not intrude.
They are not clouding
my mind
like they do at home,
I hear them,
and I wash them away

— And all it took was two days in the sun

I trod water for three years.
It's only now that I've moved on,
I look back and realise, I wasn't living,
I was just surviving

Manifesting

I am manifesting the life that I want,
because I see no other way,
because there is something so beautiful
about the idea of it,
not just because it could work,
but because I need it to work,
because I want to listen to my favourite songs
on repeat,
because I want to work hard, play hard,
because I am a dreamer and always will be,
because I'm really hoping that life is simpler
than I think it is,
because I am due a miracle,
because I am a miracle,
because I am afraid of life's uncertainty,
but words help ease my anxiety,
because nothing else can soothe me,
expect the possibility
that maybe
I could get everything I've ever wanted,
that maybe,
I even deserve it

That I lived so freely,
laughed so loudly,
loved so deeply,
let that be my legacy

A Privilege

It has taken me many years,
but I am no longer ashamed
of my own company

I am alone but not lonely,
I am without but not empty

There is no one who knows me like me,
there is no one who looks out for me like me,
there is no one who roots for me like me,
there is no one who loves me like me

Spending time with myself
is my biggest luxury

I can still
crave time for myself
and wish to find you

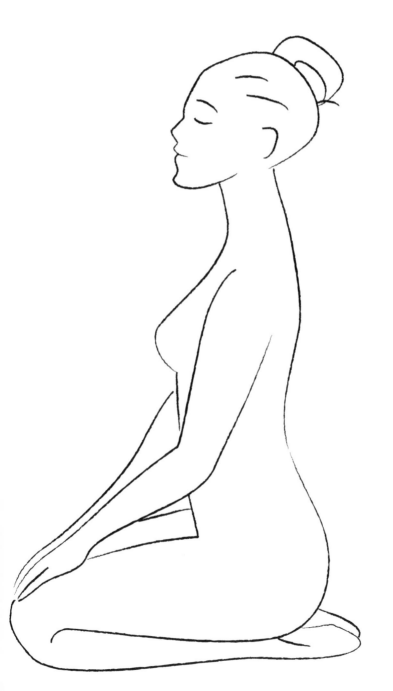

Life-long Love

I do not need love
to make me feel like my life
is worth living,
it is not the only thing
that I seek.
But oh how I want it,
oh how I crave it.
How I want
to share my laughs,
my successes,
my journey.
I want someone to see me in all my glory
and bask in it with me.
I want my story to be felt,
not just heard.
And that is why,
though I don't need you,
my God, how I want you,
oh baby, how I want you.
I want you so that we can face any darkness
together.
Just because we are strong
on our own
doesn't mean we have to be.
Together
we can take
our two beautiful lives
and let them exist
side by side,

sharing the same space,
the same time,
facing the world as a team.
Strong
because we are both strong,
everlasting
because we are both everlasting,
entwined,
interlaced
in life-long
love

In a Lifetime

You will live, my dear.
You will live,
you will live.
You will taste the sun
on your back
as you stand over
the Grand Canyon.
You will dip
your toes
in crystal blue waters in Bali.
You will dream,
and you will achieve your dream,
and then
you will get to choose
a new dream.
You will feel,
and you will love,
and you will recognise that love
in your daughter's eyes.
You will hold her hand,
keep her safe
her whole life,
and she will watch you grow old
with grace,
a constant sunset
etched
into your lips
that you will use to kiss
again and again and again.

You will live,
my darling,
you will live,
you will live,
and what a beautiful life it will be

acknowledgements

A second time around,
there is not much left to say.

But once again:

To my friends and family,
thank you for staying

To my lovers,
thank you for leaving

To my readers,
thank you for reading

To myself,
thank you for persevering

And to the one I haven't met yet,
hurry the fuck up,
I'm waiting

Thank you all for keeping my dreams alive

about the author

nieve is a 26-year-old poet and writer based in London. After receiving her bachelor of arts degree in English literature, she now continues her passion for all things writing by inspiring others as a secondary school English teacher.

In 2021, she published her debut poetry collection, *On Love and Life*, which was a culmination of her experiences and her existence so far, centring around the two most universal themes of all: love, and life itself. A year on, *Confessions of a Hopeless Dreamer* is her introspective follow up collection, with themes of love, identity, grief and sunshine permeating throughout. nieve continues to write about what she knows, but this time, is completely grounded in the self as she 'confesses' her innermost thoughts and feelings, and reflects on her position in this world.

You can find her on Instagram and all other socials at @wordsbynieve

Or visit her website at www.wordsbynieve.com

If you enjoyed this book, please consider leaving a review; they are always appreciated.